Tunisian Crochet Stitches

Gorgeous Tunisian Crochet Stitches For Beginners

Copyright © 2023

DEDICATION

Contents

Tunisian Crochet Lattice Stitch

GAUGE

The gauge varies for each square of the Tunisian Holiday Sampler Blanket. Reference the starting chain stitch multiple to make adjustments to your square. All squares should measure about 11.5" square before the border is added.

ABBREVIATIONS

2sc = 2 single crochet in the same stitch (increase made)

Ch = chain

Lts = last Tunisian stitch (see Special Stitches below)

RetP = return pass

Sc = single crochet

Sc2tog = single crochet 2 together (decrease made)

St(s) = stitch(es)

Tss = Tunisian simple stitch

Tss2tog = Tunisian simple stitch 2 together (see Special Stitches below)

SPECIAL STITCHES

Last Tunisian Stitch (Lts) – insert hook under BOTH vertical bars of the last stitch and complete as for Tunisian simple stitch

Tunisian Simple Stitch 2 Together (Tss2tog) – insert hook under the front vertical bars of the next 2 stitches, yarn over, pull up a loop through both stitches (decrease made)

STITCH MULTIPLE

Work the Tunisian Lattice Stitch over any odd number of stitches.

BORDER NOTES

To ensure that all squares of the Tunisian Holiday Sampler Blanket will join evenly, apply the Standard Border. All squares need to have 35 single crochet stitches on each size. This means you will have to increase the number of edge stitches in some cases, and decrease the number of edge stitches in other places.

To increase the number of stitches along an edge, evenly place 2sc increases along the edge where needed.

To decrease the number of stitches along an edge, evenly place sc2tog decreases along the edge where needed.

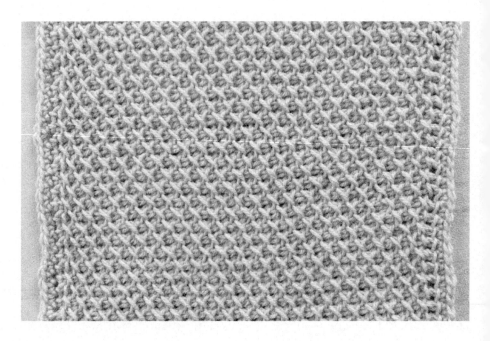

INSTRUCTIONS

ROW 1: With C and 6.5mm Tunisian crochet hook, ch 45, pull up a loop in the back bump of the 2nd ch from hook and each ch across row, RetP.

ROW 2: (Tss2tog, tss the first st of the tss2tog) across to last 2 sts, tss 1, Lts, RetP.

ROW 3: Tss 1, (tss2tog, tss the first st of the tss2tog) across to the last st, Lts, RetP.

Repeat Rows 2-3 until your square measures 11.5" tall. My square had a total of 32 rows.

Slip stitch in each vertical bar loosely to bind off. Do not cut yarn.

STANDARD BORDER

Change to 6mm crochet hook and ensure the square is facing right side up.

Ch 1 (does not count as a stitch), single crochet 35 stitches evenly across the first edge of the square, placing increases and decreases where needed. At corner, ch 2 and rotate to work along the next edge.

Single crochet 35 stitches evenly across the edge, placing increases and decreases where needed. At corner, ch 2 and rotate to work along the next edge.

Repeat Step 3 for the remaining 2 sides. At the end of the round, join with a slip stitch in the first single crochet of the round. Fasten off and block your finished square to 12" x 12".

The Tunisian Ocean Stitch

Abbreviations

Ch Chain Stitch

Tss Tunisian Simple Stitch

Tps Tunisian Purl Stitch

Sh Shell

Pattern Instructions

Foundation Chain: a multiple of 10 sts plus 2

Row 1 (rs) Fwd: Pull up loop in 2nd ch from hook and each ch across

Rtn: yo, pull through 2 loops on hook, *ch 2, yo, pull through 4 loops on hook (ch 3, sh made); rep from * to last 3 loops on hook, ch2, yo, pull through last 3 loops on hook (half sh made).

Row 2 Fwd: ch1, sk half sh, *pull up loop in next ch, pull up loop in ch btw shells on foundation ch, sk next ch, pull up loop in next ch, sk next sh; rep from * across to end, pull up loop in top of half sh

Rtn: yo, pull through 1 loop on hook, ch 1, *yo, pull through 4 loops on hook, ch 2; rep from * across to last 5 loops on hook, yo, pull through 4 loops on hook, ch 1 pull through last 2 loops on hook.

Row 3 Fwd: ch1, sk 1st vert bar, pull up loop in next ch, * sk next sh, pull up loop in next ch, pull up loop on top of sh 1 row below, sk next ch, pull up loop in next ch; rep from * across to end, sk next sh, pull up loop in next sh, sk next ch, pull up loop in last vert bar.

Rtn: yo, pull through 2 loops on hook, *ch 2, yo, pull through 4 loops on hook; rep from * across to last 3 loops on hook, ch 2, yo, pull through last 3 loops on hook.

Row 4 Fwd: ch1, sk half sh, *pull up loop in next ch, pull up loop on top of sh 1 row below, sk next ch, pull up loop in next ch, sk next sh; rep from * across to end, pull up loop in top of half sh.

Rtn: yo, pull through 1 loop on hook, ch 1, *yo, pull through 4 loops on hook, ch 2; rep from * across to last 5 loops on hook, yo, pull through 4 loops on hook, ch 1 pull through last 2 loops on hook.

Repeat rows 3 and 4 to desired length

Last row: *Insert hook into vert bar of next st, and pull through loop on hook; rep from * to end, fasten off.

Tunisian Seed Stitch Crochet

Foundation:

A: Ch an even number, sk first ch, *insert hook in next ch, yo, pull lp through, leave lp on hook, rep from * across.

B: Ch 1, [yo, pull through 2 lps on hook] across, 1 lp remains.

Row 1:

A: Sk first vertical bar, [tks in next st, trs in next st] to last st, insert hook in last st under two outer vertical bars, yo, pull lp through.

B: Ch 1, [yo, pull through 2 lps on hook] across, 1 lp remains.

Row 2:

A: Sk first vertical bar, [trs in next st, tks in next st] to last st, insert hook in last st under two outer vertical bars, yo, pull lp through.

B: Ch 1, [yo, pull through 2 lps on hook] across, 1 lp remains.

Rep rows 1-2 for pattern.

Notes: This is a nice stitch that doesn't curl as so often seen with individual stitches. An even number of chains is only required for these specific instructions. An even number isn't literally required in every application, though. If you simply stagger the different stitch on top of the other, you can use any number of chains. When working a flat swatch, I will typically make the last stitch under the two outer vertical bars for stability. It isn't a requirement and I don't use it for all applications of the same stitch pattern. It's solely a finishing technique.

Tunisian Purl Stitch

Here is our undefined row, we will be working into the front vertical bars to work the purl stitch.

As always, skip the first vertical bar that is linked to the loop on your hook. Now bring your yarn to the front of your hook as shown below.

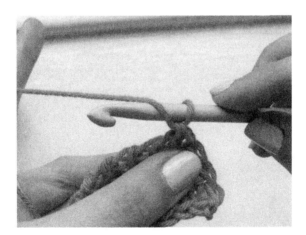

Maintaining the yarn in front, insert your hook from right to left under front vertical bar of next stitch (just as you would for Tss)

… and let the working yarn fall in front of the stitch creating a cross as you can see in the picture.

Now all that is left to do is yarn over and pull through the loop. To make things easier for you go ahead and hold the working yarn with your thumb to make it easier to pull the yarn over through.

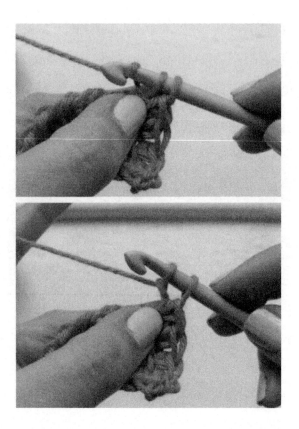

Now give it a little tug…

And move on to the next stitch, remember to bring the yarn in front of your hook before starting each stitch.

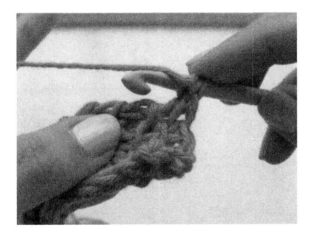

The end stitch is worked as usual, going under two loops instead of one.

And there you have it!

Tunisian Honeycomb Crochet Stitch

To start a project using Tunisian Honeycomb, you'll chain as wide as your desired piece, or pattern, dictates. I like to do the first row with Tunisian Simple crochet before starting the simple/purl repeat used throughout the rest of the pattern.

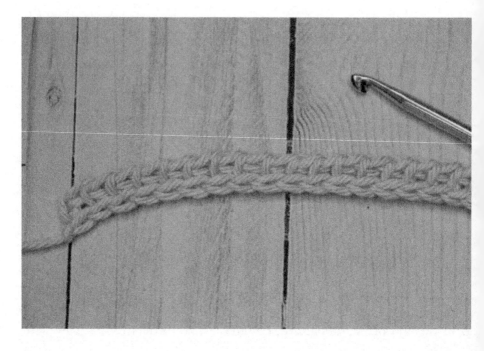

On row two, start with a Tunisian Simple Stitch (TSS) first, then do a Tunisian Purl Stitch (TPS). Alternate between the two stitches across the row. End the row by going through both sides of the last stitch from the previous row as you normally do with Tunisian.

To start your backward pass, yarn over and chain one, then yarn over and pull through two loops at a time until you reach the end.

In this photo I have the top arrows showing purl stitches (where the yarn comes from the back of the stitch) and the bottom arrows are pointing to the simple stitches (where the yarn comes straight up out of the stitch below).

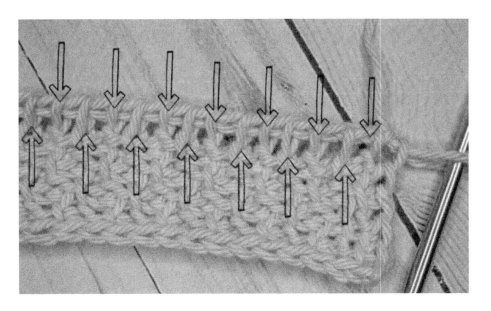

To start the next row, Tunisian Purl around the Tunisian Simple Stitch directly below, offsetting your stitches so that the simple stitches are worked into the purl stitches, and the purl stitches are worked into the simple stitches. Continue alternating in rows starting with purl then simple, purl then simple until the desired height is reached – or until your pattern tells you to stop.

Tunisian Simple Stitch Dishcloth

MATERIALS

Lily Sugar'n Cream®

(Solids: 2.5 oz/70.9 g; 120 yds/109 m; Ombres: 2 oz/56.7 g; 95 yds/86 m)

Ahoy Ombre (02019) **or** Seabreeze (01201) **or** White (00001) **or** Robin's Egg (01215)

or Tangerine (01699)   1   **ball or 42 yds/38 m**

Optional for embroidery:

Sunshine (00073)   1   **ball or 13 yds/12 m**

Tangerine (01699)   1   **ball or 3 yds/3 m**

Size U.S. J/10 (6 mm) Tunisian crochet hook **or size needed to obtain gauge.**

Optional: Large eyed blunt tapestry needle for Cross Stitch.

SIZE

Approx 8" [20.5 cm] square.

GAUGE

14 sts and 13 rows = 4" [10 cm] in Tunisian simple st (Tss).

INSTRUCTIONS

Note: Work all rows with right side of work facing.

Chain (ch) 26.

Note: Work into horizontal bumps at back of foundation chain for 1st row.

1st row: Forward pass: (Right to left).

Draw up a loop in 2nd ch from hook. Draw up a loop in each remaining (rem) ch to end of chain, leaving all loops on hook. 26 stitches (sts) on hook. Do not turn.

Return pass: (Left to right). Yarn over hook (Yoh) and draw through last loop on hook (edge st). *Yoh and draw through 2 loops on hook. Repeat (Rep) from * until 1 loop rem on hook. Do not turn.

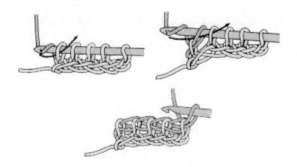

**2nd row: Forward pass: (Right to left).

*Tunisian simple st (Tss) in next st. Rep from * to end of row. Do not turn.

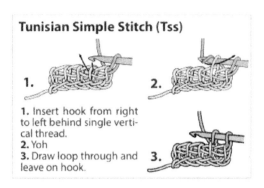

Tunisian Simple Stitch (Tss)

1.

2.

1. Insert hook from right to left behind single vertical thread.
2. Yoh
3. Draw loop through and leave on hook.

3.

Return pass: (Left to right). Yoh and draw through 1st loop on hook. *Yoh and draw through 2 loops on hook. Rep from * to end of row. 1 loop rem on hook. Do not turn.**

Rep from ** to ** until work from beginning measures approx 8" [20.5 cm], ending on return pass.

Finishing row: (Right to left). *Slip stitch (sl st) in next vertical bar. Rep from * to end of row. Fasten off.

Optional: Cross Stitch Daisy: Using Chart as reference, find center of Dishcloth and cross stitch daisy on dishcloth.

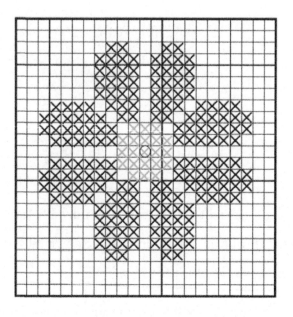

Tunisian Crochet Ear Warmer

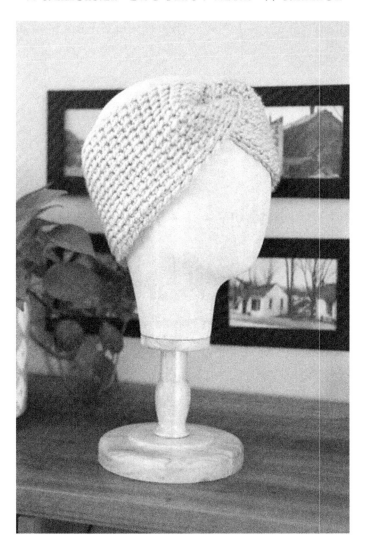

Materials:

-1 skein bulky (5) yarn, I Love This Chunky Yarn in Warm Blush (approx. 65 yds)

-6.5mm crochet hook, a straight hook without handle

-tapestry needle

-scissors

Gauge and Measurements:

Gauge: 14 sts x 9 rows = 4" square.

The finished piece measures 10.5"wide x 4.5" tall, sewn together. Gauge is only important for this project if you want to make the piece to these measurements.

Tunisian Crochet Ear Warmer Pattern:

Ch 16.

Starting in the second ch from hook, insert hook into st, yarn over and pull up a loop. Keeping that loop on the hook, insert hook into next ch and pull up another loop. Continue pulling up loops in each ch st across the row.

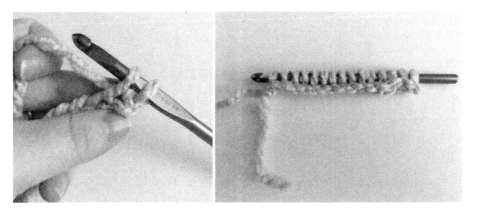

Now you will start your return pass. First, ch 1 with the first loop. Yarn over and pull through two loops.

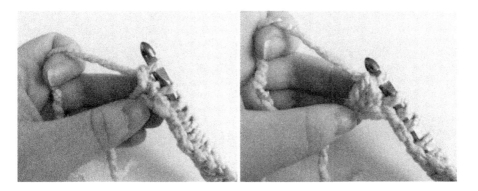

Yarn over again and pull through another 2 loops. Repeat to the end of the row.

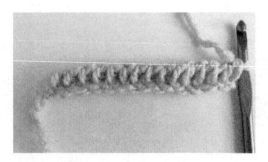

Next, begin the forward pass. You will be working this row into the vertical loops of the previous row.

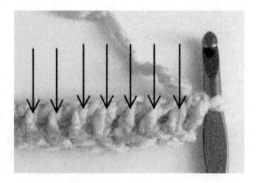

Insert the hook into the second vertical loop from the hook. Yarn over and pull up a loop.

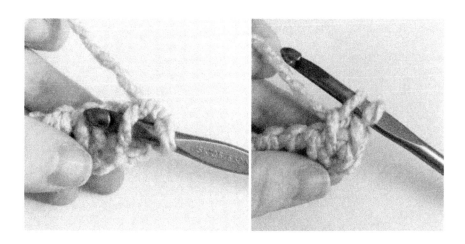

Keep the loop on the hook, and insert the hook into the next vertical loop, yarn over, pull up a loop. Repeat until the last st of the row. For the last st, insert the hook into the two loops at the end of the row. Yarn over and pull up a loop.

 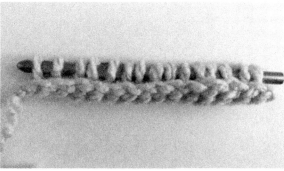

Complete another return pass. Keep stitching in this fashion, forward pass, return pass.

Create 51 rows.

For the last row, sl st into each vertical loop across the row.

Tie off leaving a long tail for sewing.

Fold the ends of the earwarmer with the right-side facing in. Place the two ends together, overlapping.

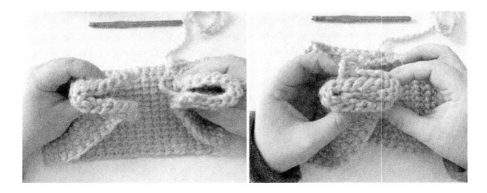

Sew together this edge, making sure to sew through each of the four layers.

Turn the piece right side out.

Enjoy your ear warmer!

Simple Striped Tunisian Crochet Blanket

SUPPLIES

2 balls of Lion Brand Wool Ease Thick and Quick Bonus Bundle in Fisherman (80% Acrylic, 20% Wool, 340g/12oz, 212yds/194m)

1 ball of each of Lion Brand Wool Ease Thick and Quick in Fisherman, Glacier, Slate (80% Acrylic, 20% Wool, 170g/6oz, 106yds/97m)

1 ball of Lion Brand Wool Ease Thick and Quick Hudson Bay (80% Acrylic, 20% Wool, 140g/5oz, 87yds/80m)

P/16 (11.5mm) Tunisian crochet hook, approx. 30-36 inches long

tapestry needle

scissors

ABBREVIATIONS

st(s) – stitch(es)

sl st – slip st

ch – chain stitch

yo – yarn over

TSS – Tunisian Simple Stitch: (forward pass) insert hook behind the front vertical bar, yarn over and bring up a loop, leaving the loop on the hook.

MC – main color – Fisherman

C1 – Slate

C2 – Hudson Bay

C3 – Glacier

NOTES

Skill level: Easy

Sizes: One size – 40in wide x 58in long

Gauge: 6 sts and 5.5 rows per 4 inches of Tunisian Simple Stitch.

At the beginning of the TSS row, you already have a loop on your hook, so you'll work the first TSS stitch by inserting your hook into the 2nd front vertical bar.

When switching colors, use the new color to complete the last stitch of the reverse pass: YO with the new color yarn and pull through the last 2 loops. This ensures the first loop of the next forward pass is in the right color.

Once you get past Row 54, you can make the blanket as long or as short as you want. Extra yarn can be used to add tassels or fringe.

Yarn is carried from one row to the next unless the pattern specifies to cut the yarn as indicated.

INSTRUCTIONS

Ch. 60.

Row 1 (Foundation row, forward): [MC] Starting from the 2nd ch from hook, *insert hook into the back bump, YO, pull up a loop, leaving the loop on the hook.* Repeat from * to complete the first forward pass. Do not turn at end of row.

Row 1 (Foundation row, reverse): [MC] YO, pull yarn through 1 loop. *YO, pull yarn through 2 loops.* Repeat from * to complete first reverse pass. Counts as first row in color chart. (60 sts)

Rows 2-6: [MC] (forward pass) TSS across row. (reverse pass) YO, pull yarn through 1 loop. *YO, pull yarn through 2 loops.* Repeat from * to complete reverse pass.

**Color change: At the end of Row 6, YO with C1 to pull through last 2 loops.

Row 7: Work TSS forward/reverse passes in C1, using MC to YO and pull through last 2 loops.

Row 8: Work TSS forward/reverse passes in MC, using C1 to YO and pull through last 2 loops.

Row 9-10: Repeat Rows 7-8. Cut MC after Row 10, leaving a 6in tail.

Rows 11-16: Work TSS forward/reverse passes in C1, using MC to YO and pull through last 2 loops of Row 16.

Row 17: Work TSS forward/reverse passes in MC, using C1 to YO and pull through last 2 loops.

Row 18: Work TSS forward/reverse passes in C1, using MC to YO and pull through last 2 loops.

Rows 19-20: Repeat Rows 17-18. Cut C1 after Row 20, leaving a 6in tail.

Rows 21-23: Work TSS forward/reverse passes in MC, using C2 to YO and pull through last 2 loops of Row 23.

Rows 24-27: Repeat Rows 7-10, replacing C1 with C2. Cut MC after Row 27, leaving a 6in tail.

Rows 28-32: Work TSS forward/reverse passes in C2, using MC to YO and pull through last 2 loops of Row 32.

Rows 33-39: Repeat Rows 17-23, replacing C1 with C2. Cut C2 after Row 36, leaving a 6in tail.

Rows 40-53: Repeat Rows 7-20, replacing C1 with C3. Cut MC after Row 43, and cut C3 after Row 53, leaving 6in tails.

Rows 54-80: Work TSS forward/reverse passes in MC.

Row 81 (Bind off): [MC] *Insert your hook under the next vertical bar, YO and pull through both the vertical bar and the loop on the hook, similar to a slip stitch.* Repeat from * to the end of the row. You should end up with 1 loop left on your hook. Cut the yarn, and pull the end through the loop to fasten off.

Finishing: Weave in all remaining ends. Pin the blanket to a flat surface and steam or wet block the edges to relax the yarn and prevent the ends from curling.

Tunisian Pyramid Lace Stitch Tutorial

Abbreviations:

ch: chain

ea: each

yo: yarn over

tks: Tunisian knit stitch

m1tb: make one in the top bar (increase)

st(s): stitch(es)

Tunisian Pyramid Lace Stitch

R1: Forward Pass: ch 17, starting in the 2nd ch from the hook, pick up a loop in ea ch across. =17 loops

Return Pass: yo and pull through 1 loop on the hook, yo and pull through 1 loop on the hook, *yo and pull through 4 loops on the hook, yo and pull through 1 loop on the hook, yo and pull through 2 loops on the hook, yo and pull through 1 loop on the hook. Repeat 2x from the * across. Yo and pull through 4 loops on the hook, yo and pull through 1 loop on the hook, yo and pull through 2 loops on the hook.

R2: Forward Pass: tks **(on hook)**, *m1tb, pick up a loop in the eye of the cluster, m1tb, tks. Repeat from the * across. =17 loops

Return Pass: yo and pull through 1 loop on the hook, yo and pull through 2 loops on the hook, yo and pull through 2 loops on the hook, *yo and pull through 1 loop on the hook, yo and pull through 4 loops on the hook, yo and pull through 1 loop on the hook, yo and pull through 2 loops on the hook. Repeat 2x. Yo and pull through 2 loops on the hook, yo and pull through 2 loops on the hook.

R3: Forward Pass: tks, tks, *tks, m1tb, pick up a loop in the eye of the cluster, m1tb. Repeat from the * across until 3 sts remain. Tks in the last 3 sts. =17 loops

Return Pass: yo and pull through 1 loop on the hook, yo and pull through 1 loop on the hook, *yo and pull through 4 loops on the hook, yo and pull through 1 loop on the hook, yo and pull through 2 loops on the hook, yo and pull through 1 loop on the hook. Repeat 2x from the * across. Yo and pull through 4 loops on the hook, yo and pull through 1 loop on the hook, yo and pull through 2 loops on the hook.

Repeat R2 and R3 until desired length and then bind off.

Tunisian Pyramid Lace Stitch Photo Tutorial

To make this Tunisian Lace Stitch start with a multiple of 4+1.

R1: Forward Pass:

1. Chain 17,

2. starting in the 2nd chain from the hook, pick up a loop in each chain across. =17 loops

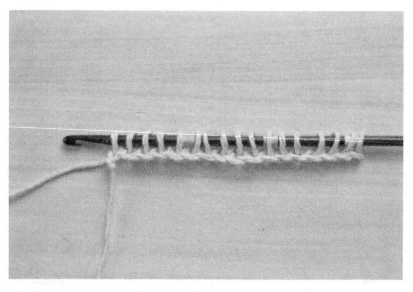

Return Pass:

3. Yarn over (image 1) and pull through 1 loop on the hook (image 2),

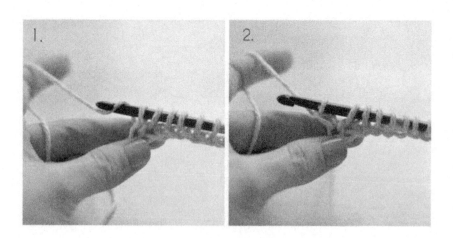

4. yarn over (image 1) and pull through 1 loop on the hook (image 2),

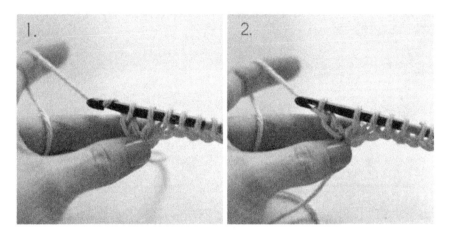

5. *yarn over (image 1) and pull through 4 loops on the hook (image 2),

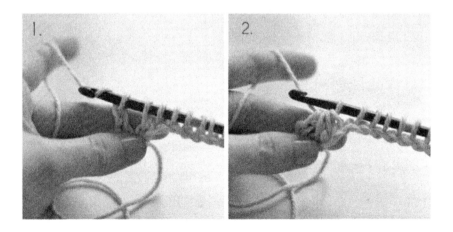

6. yarn over (image 1) and pull through 1 loop on the hook (image 2),

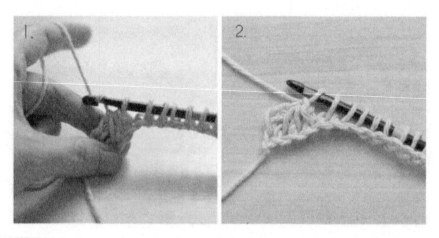

7. yarn over (image 1) and pull through 2 loops on the hook (image 2),

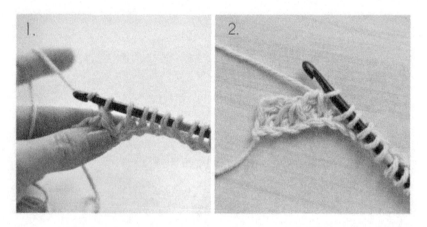

8. yarn over (image 1) and pull through 1 loop on the hook. (image 2)

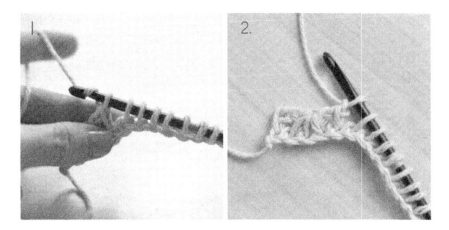

9. Repeat steps 5–8 two times.

10. Yarn over (image 1) and pull through 4 loops on the hook (image 2),

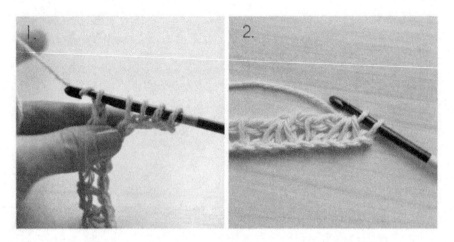

11. yarn over (image 1) and pull through 1 loop on the hook (image 2),

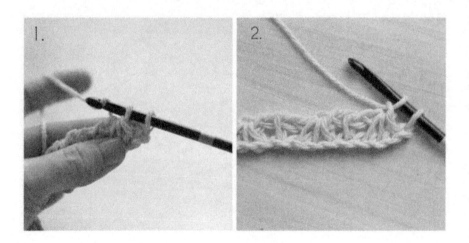

12. yarn over (image 1) and pull through 2 loops on the hook (image 2).

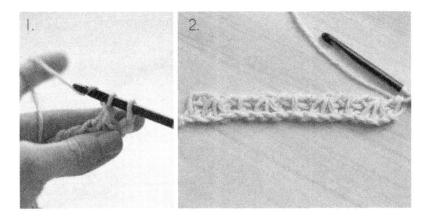

R2: Forward Pass:

13. Tunisian knit stitch or tks **(the loop on the hook counts as a tks),**

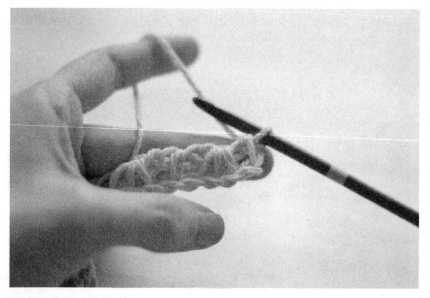

14. *Make one in the top bar or m1tb by inserting the hook into the chain space next to the hook (I like to go under both loops, not just one),

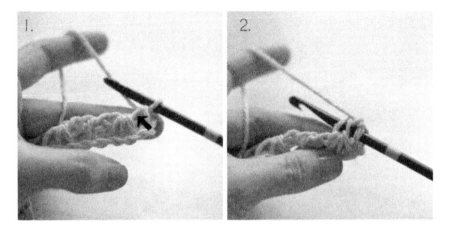

15. yarn over (image 1) and pull up a loop (image 2),

16. pick up a loop in the eye of the cluster (image 1 & 2),

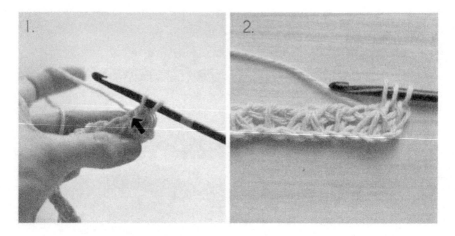

17. Make one in the top bar or m1tb,

18. Tunisian knit stitch or tks.

19. Repeat steps 14–18 three times.

Return Pass:

20. Yarn over (image 1) and pull through 1 loop on the hook (image 2),

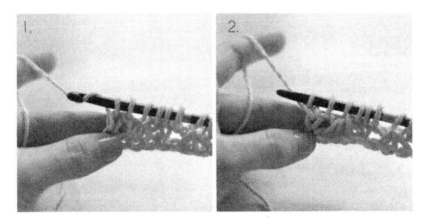

21. yarn over (image 1) and pull through 2 loops on the hook (image 2),

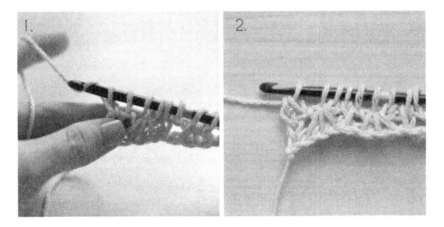

22. yarn over (image 1) and pull through 2 loops on the hook (image 2),

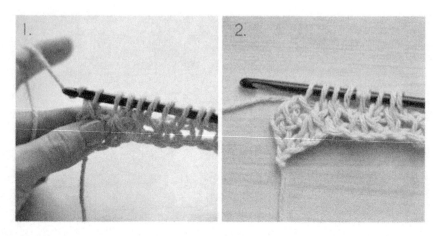

23. *yarn over (image 1) and pull through 1 loop on the hook (image 2),

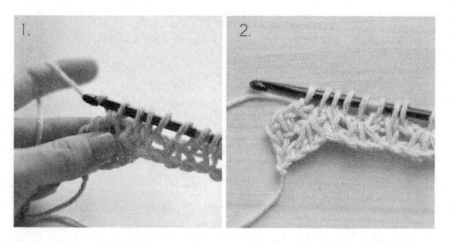

24. yarn over (image 1) and pull through 4 loops on the hook (image 2),

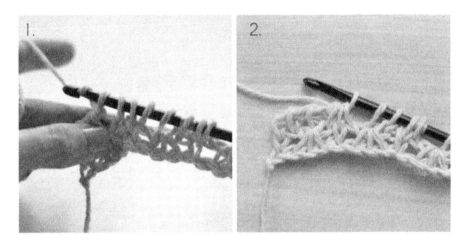

25. yarn over (image 1) and pull through 1 loop on the hook (image 2),

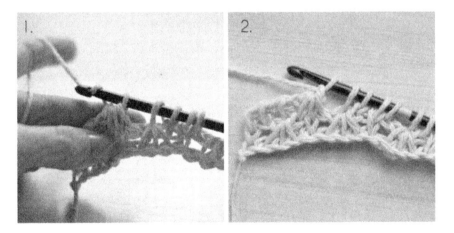

26. yarn over (image 1) and pull through 2 loops on the hook (image 2).

27. Repeat steps 23–26 two more times.

28. Yarn over (image 1) and pull through 2 loops on the hook (image 2),

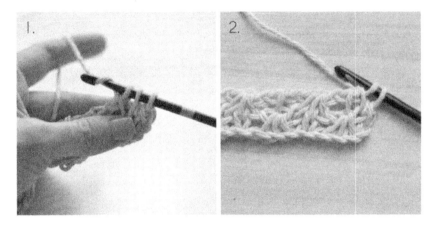

29. yarn over (image 1) and pull through 2 loops on the hook (image 2).

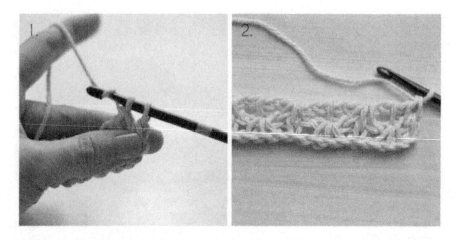

R3: Forward Pass:

30. Tunisian knit stitch or tks **(remember that this stitch is already on the hook),**

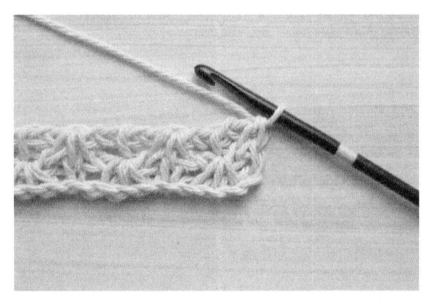

31. Tunisian knit stitch or tks,

32. *Tunisian knit stitch or tks,

33. Make one in the top bar or m1tb,

34. pick up a loop in the eye of the cluster,

35. Make one in the top bar or m1tb.

36. Repeat steps 32–35 until 3 stitches remain.

37. Tunisian knit stitch or tks in the last 3 stitches. =17 loops

Return Pass:

38. Yarn over (image 1) and pull through 1 loop on the hook (image 2),

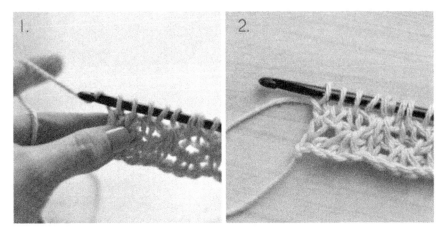

39. yarn over (image 1) and pull through 1 loop on the hook (image 2),

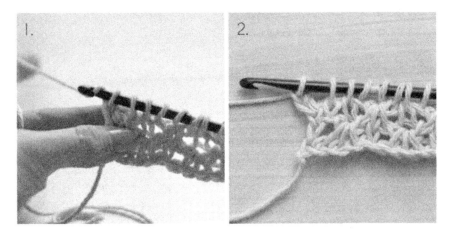

40. *yarn over (image 1) and pull through 4 loops on the hook (image 2),

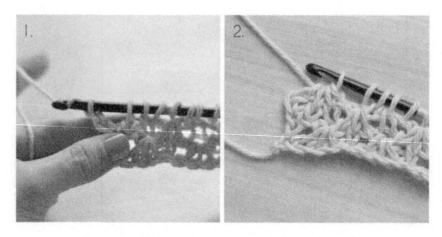

41. yarn over (image 1) and pull through 1 loop on the hook (image 2),

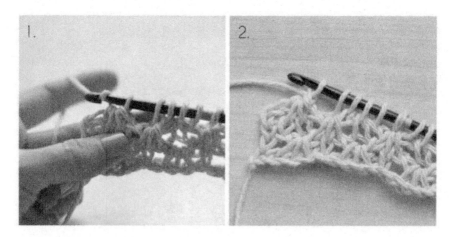

42. yarn over (image 1) and pull through 2 loops on the hook (image 2),

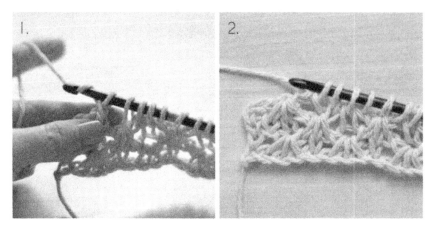

43. yarn over (image 1) and pull through 1 loop on the hook (image 2).

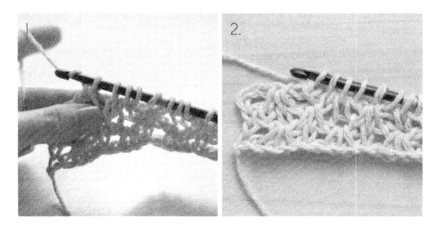

44. Repeat steps 40–43 two more times.

45. Yarn over (image 1) and pull through 4 loops on the hook (image 2),

46. yarn over (image 1) and pull through 1 loop on the hook (image 2),

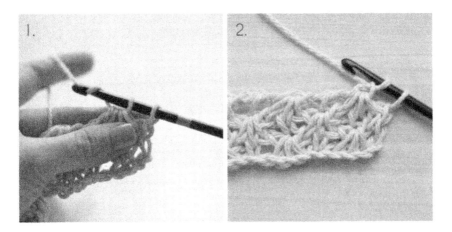

47. yarn over (image 1) and pull through 2 loops on the hook (image 2)

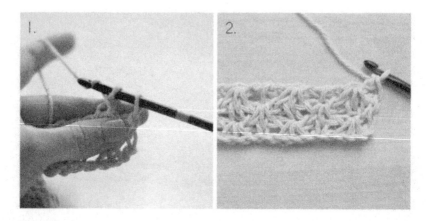

This is what your project should look like so far.

Repeat **R2** and **R3** until desired length and then bind off.

The end!

Printed in Great Britain
by Amazon

37008158R00050